TEXTURA
Sort It by TEXTURE

By Nicholas O'Hara
Traducido por Eida de la Vega

conceptos
básicos

Gareth Stevens
PUBLISHING

Agrupar significa juntar cosas que son parecidas. Puedes agrupar cosas por su textura o forma.

Sorting is putting things that are alike together. You can sort by how things feel to touch.

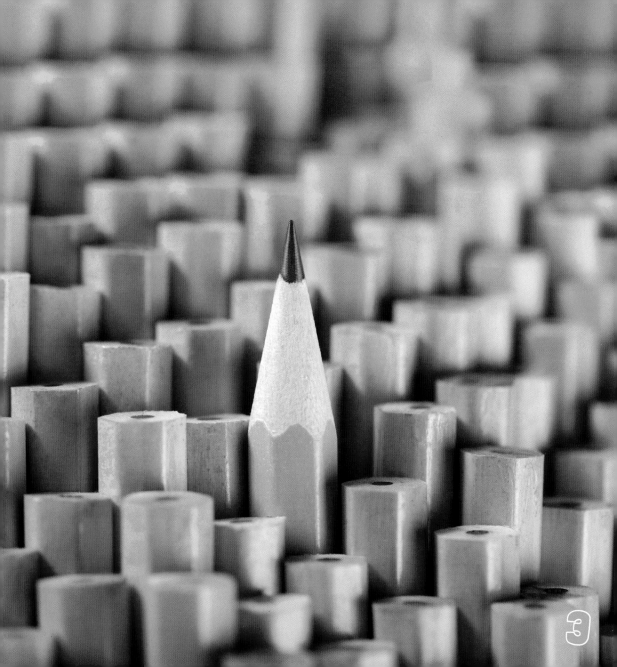

La madera puede ser lisa
o áspera.

Wood can feel smooth
or rough.

Esta madera es áspera.

- -

This wood feels rough.

Las rocas pueden ser lisas o ásperas.

Rocks can feel smooth or rough.

Estas rocas son lisas.

These rocks feel smooth.

Los juguetes pueden ser
duros o suaves.

Toys can feel hard
or soft.

Estos juguetes
son suaves.

These toys feel soft.

Los sombreros pueden
ser firmes o suaves.

Hats can feel hard
or soft.

Estos sombreros
son firmes.

These hats feel hard.

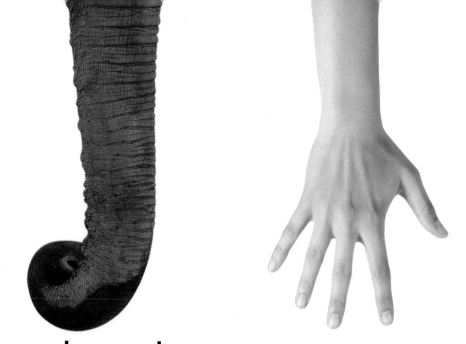

La piel puede ser áspera
o lisa.

Skin can feel bumpy
or smooth.

Esta piel es áspera.

This skin feels bumpy.

Las carreteras pueden ser
accidentadas o lisas.

Roads can feel bumpy
or smooth.

Esta carretera es lisa.

This road feels smooth.

15

La piel de la fruta puede
ser áspera o lisa.

Fruit can feel bumpy
or smooth.

Esta fruta es áspera.

This fruit feels bumpy.

Algunas golosinas son
pegajosas y otras
son secas.

Treats can feel sticky
or dry.

Estas golosinas son pegajosas.

These treats feel sticky.

La pasta puede ser seca
y firme o jugosa
y escurridiza.

Pasta can feel dry and
hard or wet and slippery.

Esta pasta es jugosa
y escurridiza.

This pasta feels wet
and slippery.

¿Cómo describirías la piel de estos animales si la tocaras?

How do you think each of these animals feels to touch?

23

Please visit our website, www.garethstevens.com. For a free color catalog of all our high-quality books, call toll free 1-800-542-2595 or fax 1-877-542-2596.

Cataloging-in-Publication Data

O'Hara, Nicholas.
Sort it by texture = Textura / by Nicholas O'Hara.
p. cm. — (Sort It out! = Vamos a agrupar por...)
Parallel title: Vamos a agrupar por...
In English and Spanish.
Includes index.
ISBN 978-1-4824-3223-7 (library binding)
1. Materials — Texture — Juvenile literature. I. O'Hara, Nicholas. II. Title.
TA418.7 O43 2016
620.1'1292—d23

First Edition

Published in 2016 by
Gareth Stevens Publishing
111 East 14th Street, Suite 349
New York, NY 10003

Copyright © 2016 Gareth Stevens Publishing

Designer: Sarah Liddell
Editor: Therese Shea
Spanish Translation: Eida de la Vega

Photo credits: Cover, p. 1 (polka dots) Victoria Kalinina/Shutterstock.com; cover, p. 1 (fruit) Valentyn Volkov/Shutterstock.com; p. 3 Stocksnapper/Shutterstock.com; p. 4 (left) Evlakhov Valeriy/Shutterstock.com; p. 4 (right) PhotographyByMK/Shutterstock.com; p. 5 Opas Chotiphantawanon/Shutterstock.com; p. 6 Perfkos/Shutterstock.com; p. 7 Apollofoto/Shutterstock.com; p. 8 Poznyakov/Shutterstock.com; p. 9 MAii Thitikorn/Shutterstock.com; p. 10 (left) Alex Staroseltsev/Shutterstock.com; p. 10 (right) Lucy Liu/Shutterstock.com; p. 11 stockphoto mania/Shutterstock.com; p. 12 (elephant trunk) Aaron Amat/Shutterstock.com; p. 12 (hand) Antonio Guillem/Shutterstock.com; p. 13 Anan Kaewkhammul/Shutterstock.com; p. 14 AlexanderZam/Shutterstock.com; p. 15 Twenty20 Inc/Shutterstock.com; p. 16 margouillat/Shutterstock.com; p. 17 Viktar Malyshchyts/Shutterstock.com; p. 18 (marshmallows) Texturis/Shutterstock.com; pp. 18 (candy), 21 Africa Studio/Shutterstock.com; p. 19 de2marco/Shutterstock.com; p. 20 (left) nelik/Shutterstock.com; p. 20 (right) motorolka/Shutterstock.com; p. 23 (main) Eric Isselee/Shutterstock.com; p. 23 (turtle) Zorandim/Shutterstock.com.

Printed in the United States of America

CPSIA compliance information: Batch #CS15GS: For further information contact Gareth Stevens, New York, New York at 1-800-542-2595.